Ransom Neutron Stars
Gaps in the Brain
by Jill Atkins

Published by Ransom Publishing Ltd.
Unit 7, Brocklands Farm, West Meon, Hampshire GU32 1JN, UK
www.ransom.co.uk

ISBN   978 178591 433 1
First published in 2017

Gaps
in the Brain

Jill Atkins

There is an illness that cannot be seen. It is an illness of the brain.

Something attacks part of the brain. Then that part of the brain cuts out.

The illness is hard to spot.

In the beginning it seems nothing is wrong. You might just forget little things. You might forget the name of your cat, or your friends.

Everybody forgets the name of a friend sometimes.

If you forget a name, is it just a bad memory? Or are you getting gaps in your brain?

When you get this illness, you might forget things.

You might forget how to cook.

May forgot to put the eggs in the cake mix.

You might forget what to get at the shops.

Ted forgot to get his fish for supper.

You might forget where your home is.

Damini got lost on the way home.

You might forget where things are kept.

Jack put the milk back in the dishwasher.

You might find it hard to say the right words.

Veer called his dog a teapot.

Sometimes it can be very funny. You and your friends will laugh.

But sometimes it can be sad. Then your friends will support you and help you.

If you have this illness, you must see a doctor.

The doctor will tell you that you must have some tests.

They will be tests of your brain.

The tests might be a CT scan or an MRI scan.

The tests will take place at a hospital or a clinic.

For the tests, you will need to rest on a bed. The bed will move inside a big long hoop.

You might not like to go into the hoop, but it is OK. It will not harm you. In fact, it will help you.

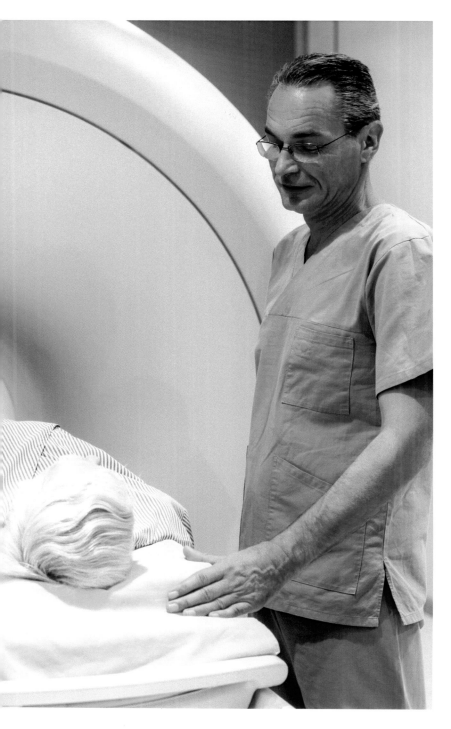

The doctor can see the part of the brain that is sick.

He can see what is happening in the brain. He can see if there are any gaps in the brain.

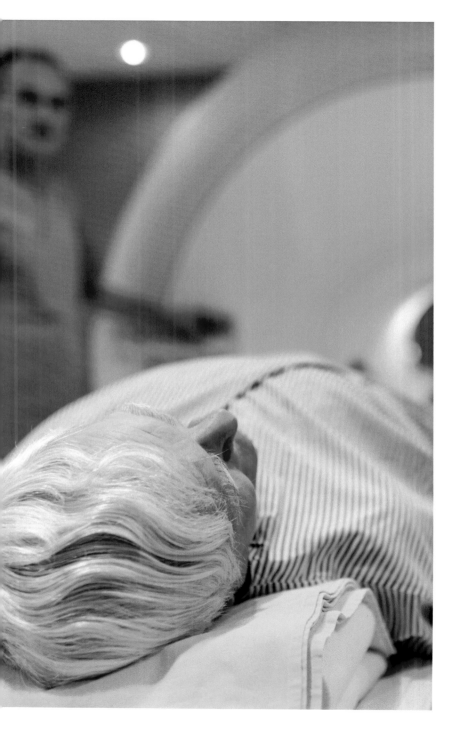

If you have gaps in the brain, it can be hard to treat this illness.

Maybe you can have some pills. Sometimes they help the illness – but sometimes they have no effect.

But you can get help and you can still
have fun.

There are lots of things you can still do.

If you like to do sport, you can still do
sport.

If you like to swim, you can still swim.

If you like to walk with friends, you can still walk with friends.

You can still go out if you have someone to go with you. Then it's no problem.

Remember – if you have gaps in the brain, you can still enjoy your life.

You are not on your own. Your friends can help you. In fact, your friends will want to help you!

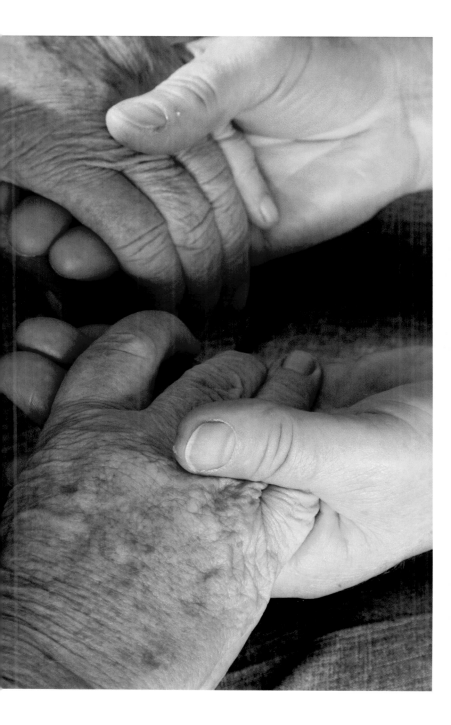

There are good things too.

If you forget your keys one day …

… nobody can blame you. After all, you have gaps in the brain!

Have you read?

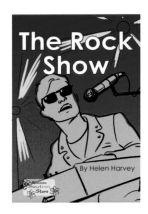

The Rock Show

by Helen Harvey

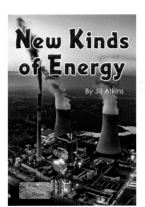

New Kinds of Energy

by Jill Atkins

Have you read?

G B H

by Jill Atkins

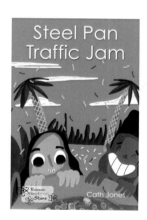

Steel Pan Traffic Jam

by Cath Jones

Ransom Neutron Stars

Gaps in the Brain
Word count **489**

Covers:
Letters and Sounds Phase 5

Phonics

Phonics 1	Not Pop, Not Rock Go to the Laptop Man Gus and the Tin of Ham		*Phonics 2*	Deep in the Dark Woods Night Combat Ben's Jerk Chicken Van
Phonics 3	GBH Steel Pan Traffic Jam Platform 7		*Phonics 4*	The Rock Show **Gaps in the Brain** New Kinds of Energy

Book bands

Pink	Curry! Free Runners My Toys		*Red*	Shopping with Zombies Into the Scanner Planting My Garden
Yellow	Fit for Love The Lottery Ticket In the Stars		*Blue*	Awesome ATAs Wolves The Giant Jigsaw
Green	Fly, May FLY! How to Start Your Own Crazy Cult The Care Home		*Orange*	Text Me The Last Soldier Best Friends